COSTUME of ANCIENT GREECE

DAVID J SYMONS

drawings by Jack Cassin-Scott

B T Batsford Limited   *London*

For Pamela

First published 1987

Typeset by Tek-Art Ltd, Kent
and printed in Great Britain by
Anchor Brendon Ltd,
Tiptree, Essex
for the publishers
B T Batsford Limited
4 Fitzhardinge Street
London W1H 0AH

British Library Cataloguing in
Publication Data
Symons, David J.
  Costume of Ancient Greece.
  1. Costume — Greece
  I. Title
  391'.00938   GT550

ISBN 0 7134 5325 7

Contents

THRACE

MACEDONIA

THESSALY

AEGEAN SEA

Troy

LESBOS

LYDIA

AKARNANIA

OZOLIAN
LOKRIS

PHOKIS

7 ✗

BOIOTIA

✗ 2

✗ 5

EUBOIA

IONIA

Sardis

ACHAIA

Megara

✗ 3

Athens

Teos

ARKADIA

6 ✗

Mycenae

✗

4

Olympia

P
E
L
O
P
O
N
N
E
S
E

Argos

AIGINA

Miletos

CARIA

Sparta

Pylos

LAKONIA

AMORGOS

KOS

RHODES

Battles ✗

1 Thermopylai
2 Plataia
3 Marathon
4 Salamis
5 Mykalessos
6 Lechaion
7 Chaironeia

CRETE

Knossos

1   The Greek homeland

1 Setting the scene

Our picture of Greek dress is built up from a number of sources. Only a few fragments of the textiles themselves have survived, most notably some fifth and fourth century examples in a tomb at Kertch in the Crimea. We are therefore forced to rely on secondary sources for our information.

Something can be gleaned from the written evidence. For the Mycenaean Bronze Age we have clay tablets written in the Linear B script which give us insights, albeit hard to interpret, into the production of textiles at that time. From the eighth century onwards the works of contemporary writers contain references of varying use. These, however, tend to be scattered asides in poetry and drama or brief allusions or comments in historical works rather than connected accounts. A few later (Roman period) writers preserve fuller information which seems to be derived from now lost Hellenistic sources.

Our main sources of information therefore are the artistic products of the Greeks – terracotta figurines, large and small stone and metal sculptures, the rare wall-paintings and mosaics and, above all, the pottery vases with figured decoration that were produced from the eighth to the fourth century. However, a word of caution is required about the nudity or near nudity frequently found in Greek art. Although the Greeks were remarkably unprudish about the human body it is likely that this nudity actually reflects artistic interest in the naked body and artistic convention. No one is likely to have walked the streets of Athens stark naked.

At one time or another Greeks were to be found living in places as far apart as Spain and India, southern Russia and Egypt. Obviously there must have been marked differences in fashion from place to place as a result both of climate and of the influence of the varied peoples whom the Greeks had as neighbours. Regrettably we have very little evidence for such local variations in dress. Even within the purely Greek regions some areas were leaders of fashion while others were considerably more backward. For the eighth to fourth centuries our evidence comes overwhelmingly from a restricted area of central Greece, and particularly from Athens. This bias in the evidence is naturally reflected in this book.

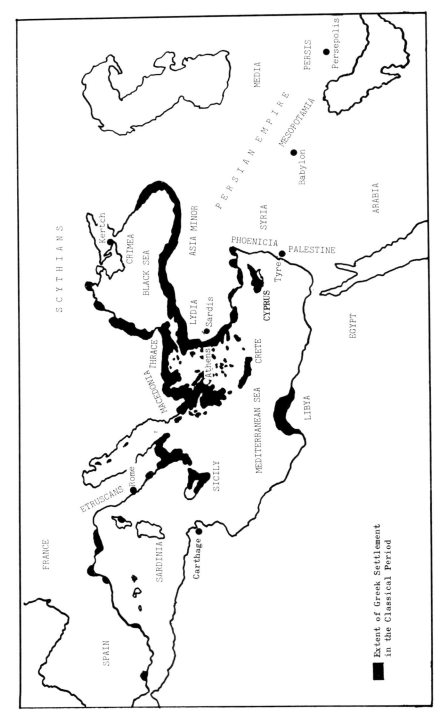

2 The Greek world

6

Materials

Wool (*erion*) and linen (*linon*) were used from the Mycenaean period onwards and probably accounted for the vast majority of Greek clothes. Both were produced in a variety of qualities.

Other materials were, however, used to make clothing, at least after the Mycenaean period. Hemp (*kannabis*) produced very coarse cloths. Silk (*serikon*) was also known. Aristotle, writing in the fourth century, describes the manufacture of wild silk on the island of Kos and a fragment of this material was discovered in the tomb at Kertch already mentioned. It is possible, but uncertain, that the finer cultivated silk was imported, ultimately from China. Cotton is mentioned as early as the fifth century when Herodotos describes it as *eirion apo xylou* ('wool from a tree').

In addition to textiles leather, together with animal skins, was sometimes used for clothing. It was also used to make footwear.

Technology

Throughout the period covered by this book wool was spun by hand using a distaff to hold the wool and a weighted spindle to pull out and twist the thread (figure 3). Linen thread was spun in the same way after the fibres had been extracted from the flax plants.

Once prepared, the threads were woven on an upright loom (*histos*) with the warp threads weighted by heavy loom-weights. Figure 3, taken from a late sixth century pot, shows such a loom in action. Weaving has begun at the top of the loom and the weavers are working standing up. The already finished cloth can be seen rolled up at the top of the loom. The woman at the left is pushing up the last weft thread. Her companion is passing a rod through the warps to separate them ready for the next weft. The shuttle, which threaded the weft through, has been jammed between the warps while not in use.

Using such a loom a variety of fabrics could be produced and even very complex figured patterns were woven. Alternatively decoration might be embroidered or even painted on to the cloth with dye. All three techniques appear on the fragments from Kertch. Clothes could also be enriched by weaving in gold threads or by sewing on decorative plaques of beaten gold.

Felt making was also practised, particularly for the manufacture of hats.

Colour

Cheap wool and linen clothes might be left in their natural colours. For wool this meant not only white but also a range of shades through off-whites, yellows, browns and red-browns to grey and black, depending on the breed of sheep. Alternatively both woollens and linens might be bleached or dyed.

Bleaching was carried out using sulphur fumes and was more common than dyeing for linens. Dyes (*pharmaka*) were derived from animal, vegetable and mineral sources and produced a variety of colours. Wool

3   Women spinning wool and weaving

was usually dyed before it was woven, either as fleece or as yarn. A mordant was used to give fast, even colours and manipulation of the amounts of dye or mordant or of the dyeing time allowed a range of shades to be produced.

Purple dye was made from the secretions of the shellfish *Murex brandaris*, while reds came from a beetle (*Coccus ilicis*) or from the root of the madder (*Rubiae radix*). Yellows were derived from saffron or from *Reseda luteola*, a herbaceous plant. Greens were probably produced using copper carbonate. Blue dye seems to have been made from imported indigo and black from iron salts mixed with oak tannin.

Supply

The Minoan and Mycenaean palaces clearly acted as co-ordinators of large scale textile production. The evidence of the Linear B tablets is particularly striking. Those found at Knossos mention a total of almost 100,000 sheep, mostly castrated rams kept for their wool. From the Pylos tablets comes evidence for large groups of female slaves based throughout the kingdom. These included spinners, weavers and other textile workers. The tablets mention five hundred such women as working in Pylos itself. Although the evidence is less clear it is possible that linen was also being produced on a large scale. This special interest in textiles suggests that they were being made for royal use and probably also for export. Outside of the palaces the lower classes presumably made their own clothing on a local basis.

In later times wool-working was the traditional female occupation in all walks of life. In the *Odyssey* even queens are shown weaving. However, the more high-quality and elaborate textiles would have been produced by specialists.

Certain places were famous for the production of particular kinds of textiles – Miletos for woollens, Kos for its wild silk and Amorgos for an extremely fine quality linen called *amorgis*. We also know that luxury cloth was imported from Persia, Phoenicia and Egypt. Linen was also imported from Egypt and cotton from Egypt, Arabia and India.

A note on names and dates

Throughout this book the Greek forms of the names of people, places and things have been given except where other forms are so familiar to English speakers that this would cause unnecessary confusion. For example, Herodotos and Lechaion are used rather than the latinised Herodotus and Lechaeum, but Thucydides and Athens rather than the more technically correct Thoukydides and Athenai. All dates given are BC unless otherwise stated.

Chronological Table

(Including persons named in the text)

c2200-1900	Arrival of the Greeks in Greece
c1930-1450	Minoan civilization on Crete
c1600-1200	Mycenaean civilization in mainland Greece
c1200	Collapse of Mycenaean civilization. Followed by Greek Dark Age. Greek settlements established on eastern seaboard of Asia Minor and in Cyprus
c800-700	Dark Age ends. Greece now divided into many small city-states ruled by aristocracies. Renewed contacts with eastern Mediterranean lead to greater sophistication in Greece and to reintroduction of writing. Greek colonies planted around shores of Mediterranean. Poems of Homer composed, probably in Ionia
c700	Hesiod of Askra in Boiotia, poet
c630	Alkman, poet, writing at Sparta
c575	Sappho of Lesbos, poetess
c570-500	Anakreon of Teos, poet
546	Cyrus, King of Persia (559-29) defeats Croesus, King of Lydia (c560-46) and conquers Asia Minor. Greek cities of coast brought under Persian rule
c530	Thespis of Athens, tragic playwright
c525	Cambyses, King of Persia (529-22) conquers Cyprus
510	Democracy established at Athens
499-494	Greeks of Ionia and Cyprus revolt against Darius, King of Persia (522-486). Some mainland Greeks help rebels but revolt is crushed

490	First Persian invasion of Greece defeated at Marathon
480-479	Second invasion of Greece by Xerxes, King of Persia (486-65). Battles of Thermopylai, Salamis and Plataia. Persians defeated. Simultaneous invasion of Sicily by Carthaginians defeated by Greeks at Himera
478-431	Athens builds up a sea-based empire; Sparta strongest power on land. Constant friction between them. Flowering of Greek culture, especially at Athens. Aeschylus (c525-456), Sophocles (c496-406), Euripides (c485-406), tragic playwrights; Herodotos (c484-430), historian; Pheidias (c490-430), sculptor
431-404	Peloponnesian War between Athens and Sparta. Athens defeated but both sides exhausted. Aristophanes (c445-385), comic playwright; Socrates (469-399), philosopher; Thucydides (c460-400), soldier and historian; Alkibiades (c450-404), soldier and statesman
396-340	Constant wars in Greece between city-states. In Sicily and Italy Carthaginians and Italian peoples encroach on areas settled by Greeks. Plato (c429-347), Aristotle (c384-22), philosophers; Xenophon (c428-354), soldier and historian; Iphikrates (c415-353), soldier

338	Philip II, King of Macedonia (359-336) crushes Greek opposition at battle of Chaironeia, ends real independence of city states
336	Philip II murdered. Alexander the Great, King of Macedonia (336-323)
334	Alexander invades and conquers Persian Empire
323	Alexander dies at Babylon
323-280	Alexander's generals fight among themselves. His empire is divided between three kingdoms based on Macedonia, Syria, and Egypt. Large scale Greek settlement in newly conquered lands. Menander (*c* 343-291), comic playwright; Theokritos (*c* 300-260), poet
241	Romans conquer Greeks of Sicily
214-205, 200-197	Romans defeat Philip V, King of Macedonia (221-179)
192-190	Romans defeat Antiochos III, King of Syria (223-187)
171-168	Romans defeat Perseus, King of Macedonia (179-168). Macedonia divided into small units under Roman supervision
146	Greece and Macedonia become Roman provinces
133	Eastern Asia Minor becomes Roman province
64	Syria becomes Roman province
30	Egypt, the last independent Greek state, becomes Roman province
c **AD 150-180**	Pausanias, traveller and geographer; Julius Pollux, scholar

2 Minoans and Mycenaeans

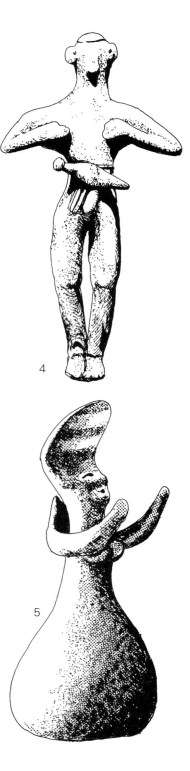

The Greeks probably arrived in what was to become Greece in the years around 2000. At about the same time Europe's first civilization developed on the island of Crete. There the non-Greek Minoans built luxurious palaces like that found at Knossos. In these palaces the Minoan ruling class lived comfortable lives supported by the products of the well-ordered Minoan society.

In the sixteenth century the Mycenaean Greeks of the mainland came under increasing Minoan influence and developed their own version of this palace-based civilization. Palaces have been excavated at sites such as Pylos, Mycenae and Tiryns. When Minoan Crete collapsed in the fifteenth century Mycenaeans established themselves in control of the palace at Knossos as well. The Mycenaeans kept administrative records in a script known as Linear B. This has been deciphered and the records, written in an early form of Greek, give us valuable information on the period.

In the late thirteenth century many Mycenaean sites were destroyed and the palace civilization collapsed. The art of writing was lost and Greece slipped into a poorly known and impoverished Dark Age. During this period many Greeks migrated to the eastern seaboard of Asia Minor and to Cyprus.

The Minoans

The earliest evidence for Minoan clothing consists of small clay and stone figures deposited in sanctuaries in about 2000. Both men and women are represented. The men are naked but for a belt and a cod-piece (figure 4). Evidence from later wall paintings and sculptures suggests that this cod-piece was quite stiff and it may have been made out of soft leather, although wool and linen are also possibilities. In their belts the men often carry daggers with broad triangular blades.

The women are dressed in flowing floor-length skirts which occasionally have flounces like those shown in wall paintings from the later palaces

4 Figurine of a Minoan man wearing a cod-piece, *c* 2000 BC

5 Figurine of a Minoan woman in a long skirt, *c* 2000 BC

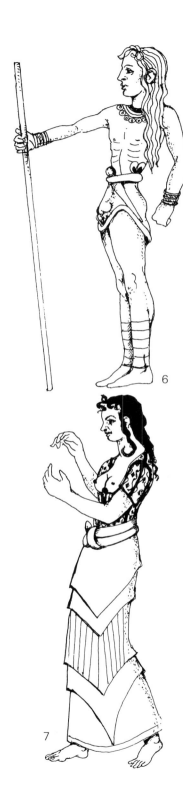

(figure 5). Although they sometimes appear to be naked above the waist other figures clearly show them wearing tight-fitting bodices which leave the breasts bare. These bodices frequently rise to form a high peaked collar behind the head (figure 5). Often a bulky belt is shown wrapped around the waist.

Both sexes sport a variety of hats and hairstyles but men usually wear their hair short and are either bare-headed or have flat beret-like hats (figure 4). Women's hair was worn long and many figures have it piled into a tall top-knot bound up with a band. Others have a towering tiara-like hat rising above their heads (figure 5).

The great palaces and other sites of the period from c 1900 to c 1450 have produced much more evidence but even so some points remain unclear. Almost all this evidence portrays members of the ruling class and we cannot be sure what Minoan commoners wore. Furthermore, many representations seem to show deities or priests and priestesses and we may not be justified in using these to interpret secular clothing.

Bearing these limitations in mind it would seem that men of this period wore two basic types of costume, the kilt and the apron. The kilt (colour plate 1) reached the thighs at the rear but came to the knees at the front, often ending there in a long tassel. The apron took two forms, double and single. The double apron (figure 6) reached to the thighs, dipping rather lower at the back than at the front. It was cut away at the sides. In many cases it is clear that it was worn over a cod-piece like that described earlier. The single apron (colour plate 1) is similar but lacks the front half and the cod-piece shows clearly. Both kilt and apron were held up by a decorated belt, presumably made of leather, which often bulges noticeably suggesting that it was padded. Occasionally men appear wearing only the cod-piece as shown in figure 4.

Almost all the surviving representations show Minoan women dressed in a long flared skirt and a tight-fitting bodice (figures 7 and 8). The skirt is generally but not always flounced. These flounces are usually held to represent horizontal strips sewn on to a skirt but it is possible that the skirt was actually built up of a number of strips sewn together and overlapping each other. Covering the junction of the skirt and the bodice is a belt. This appears either in thick padded forms or in others suggesting that they might be made of metal.

The bodice is laced across the abdomen but leaves the breasts exposed. It has short sleeves. Surviving representations make it clear that it was sewn together from a number of panels. This tailoring produced the

6   Minoan man wearing a double apron over a cod-piece

7   Minoan woman wearing a flounced skirt and bodice

figure-hugging effect that the bodice displays. On some statuettes (figure 8) a male double apron is worn over the skirt but since all these figures seem to represent goddesses or priestesses it is likely that this combination had a special significance.

Both male and female clothing could be lavishly decorated. The style of this decoration suggests that both weaving and embroidery were used.

In a number of scenes both men and women wear clothes which are clearly made of skins. These clothes include long skirts, wraps and short capes (figure 9). In every case, however, the scenes seem to show a ceremony of some kind taking place and these skin garments are presumably therefore of ceremonial or religious significance.

Both sexes often wore their hair long although men are sometimes shown with shorter hair (figure 9). Beards and moustaches are rare but do sometimes appear. Women's hair was often worn in very elaborate styles. An assortment of hats are shown. Some are simple round caps, others amazingly elaborate (figure 8) and probably religious or ceremonial rather than for everyday wear. At home, and often out of doors as well, it was common to go barefoot but a variety of boots and sandals are represented (figure 9; colour plate 1). Some men have bands rather like puttees wound around their legs as well (figure 6). Both men and women wore jewellery which included hair ornaments, earrings, necklaces and bracelets.

8 Minoan goddess wearing the male double apron over her skirt and an elaborate hat

9 Minoan man dressed in a skin cape

The Mycenaeans

It is important to remember that the Mycenaeans were very heavily influenced by the Minoans. One result of this was that many scenes in Mycenaean art were of a very Minoan character. We ought therefore to be careful not to assume that the Minoan elements in these scenes actually represent the reality of Mycenaean life. This is true of clothing among many other things.

Unfortunately it is often very difficult, if not impossible, to draw a firm distinction. This is particularly the case with female dress. Much of our evidence shows women dressed in what is basically Minoan costume – a long, flared skirt, usually with flounces, together with an open, short-sleeved bodice. Very often, however, the bodice is worn over a white bib or blouse which modestly covers the breasts (figure 10; colour plate 1). In a few cases the breasts are exposed in the Minoan manner.

10 Mycenaean woman in Minoan style dress

Most of the scenes in which this style of dress occurs seem to represent ceremonial occasions of one sort or another in the Mycenaean palaces. It is therefore possible that the dress portrayed is one that artistic convention regarded as the 'correct' one for such settings. However, the presence of the bib suggests that we are dealing with a real contemporary costume which it might be best to regard as a form of court dress. Other evidence suggests that for less formal occasions, and presumably outside the palaces, women wore a long tunic with short sleeves that was girdled at the waist (figure 11; colour plate 1).

Mycenaean men seem normally to have worn a short-sleeved, thigh-length tunic which was also girdled at the waist (figure 12). However, other figures appear dressed only in a short, flaring kilt or in what appear to be short trunks, usually decorated with rows of tassels or fringes (figure 13). Some men wear long tunics like those worn by women but these figures seem to represent priests, poets and others taking part in ceremonies of some sort, so we are probably best in regarding this as a special form of dress. Very occasionally Mycenaean art shows men dressed in Minoan costume but, as explained earlier, this may not be a valid reflection of Mycenaean use.

We know very little about cloaks or wraps in the Mycenaean period but sturdy metal pins have been found which were probably used to fasten cloaks. It is possible that the *pharwea* mentioned on the Linear B tablets may be a large woollen cloak. A fringed shawl is shown on one ivory carving from Mycenae, where it is shared by two women (colour plate 1).

Both sexes seem frequently to have gone barefoot but they also wore a variety of sandals and boots. A number of men are shown wearing white leggings of some kind wrapped around their lower legs (figure 12). These were presumably made of linen.

Although some Mycenaean men are shown with long hair in the Minoan style (figure 12), in most cases it was worn fairly short (figure 13). Older men often wore beards but moustaches seem to have been fairly unusual. Women always wore their hair long. In some cases it was dressed into very elaborate styles and bound up with ribbons (figure 10). Mycenaean jewellery was similar to that of the Minoans.

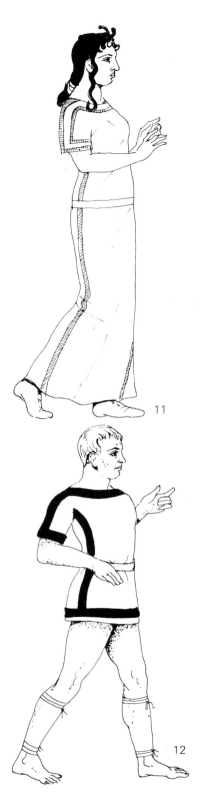

11   Mycenaean woman wearing a long belted tunic

12   Mycenaean man in a short tunic and leggings

Military dress

The Minoan warrior was armed with a sword, dagger, long thrusting spear, bow or sling. There is no direct evidence for body armour on Crete until the Mycenaeans had taken contol there in *c* 1450 and it is possible that before that date the Minoans relied solely on helmets and shields for defence.

The earliest helmets found on Crete date to the time of Mycenaean control but earlier representations suggest that the traditional Minoan helmet type was a conical cap, presumably made of leather or of leather sheathed in bronze. Shields were probably made of hide stretched over a wooden or wicker frame. They seem to have been of two types, both large enough to cover almost the whole body. One of these was convex and shaped like a figure-of-eight (see figure 13). The other, known as a 'tower shield', was semi-cylindrical and had a curved top (figure 14). Both had a long strap fixed inside which allowed them to be hung over the shoulder, leaving both hands free.

Like the Minoans the Mycenaeans were armed with swords, daggers, long thrusting spears, bows and slings. There is some evidence to suggest that body armour made either of padded linen or of linen reinforced with metal plates was worn. One complete suit of armour made up of bronze plates laced together with leather thongs has actually been found in a tomb at Dendra, near Mycenae (colour plate 1). The Dendra warrior was also equipped with bronze greaves for his legs and what seems to have been a bronze protector for his lower arm. Greaves probably made of padded linen are also shown in a number of representations (figure 13).

The Dendra burial also contained a specimen of the famous Mycenaean boars' tusk helmet (colour plate 1). These helmets were made by splitting the tusks lengthways and lacing them in horizontal rows over a sub-structure made up of vertical leather straps. The tops of these straps projected and formed a kind of tuft at the top of the helmet. Other helmets seem to have been made of bronze plates fixed to a leather cap while an all-bronze helmet has been found on Crete. Both the boars' tusk and bronze helmets are conical in shape and have bronze cheek-pieces attached. They might sometimes be fitted with decorative crests or plumes.

At first the Mycenaeans used both the figure-of-eight (figure 13) and the tower shield (figure 14) but these seem to have gone out of fashion by *c* 1400. They were replaced by much smaller round shields, possibly as a result of influence from the countries around the eastern Mediterranean.

13   Mycenaean warrior dressed in fringed trunks and carrying a figure-of-eight shield

14   Minoan warrior carrying a tower shield

3   Dress in the Archaic Period:

The eighth to sixth centuries

Because the Greeks of the time produced no figurative art and had lost the art of writing we are almost wholly ignorant of the appearance of Greek clothing between the twelfth and the eighth centuries. Despite this, however, we can see that major changes must have occurred during this period. By the eighth century the tightly-fitting tailored female clothes of the Bronze Age had been replaced by looser garments that were draped or pinned in place on the body. The archaeologically recorded appearance of pairs of long dress pins in graves of the late eleventh century probably marks this change in fashion.

In the eighth century representations of the human figure reappear in art. At first they are shown in a highly stylized form (figure 15) but more realistic representations begin in the seventh century.

15   Highly stylized eighth century figures of a man in a long *chiton* and *chlaina* and a woman in a *peplos*

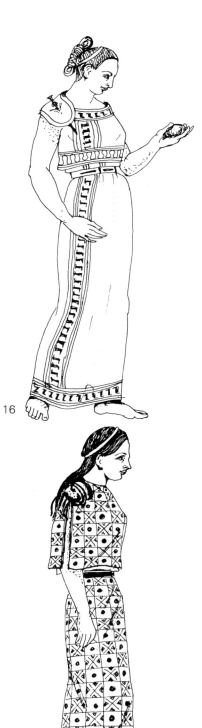

The *Iliad* and the *Odyssey* are the earliest surviving works of Greek literature. Composed by Homer, probably towards the end of the eighth century, they tell the story of the Greeks' war against Troy and its aftermath. They are set centuries before, in the Mycenaean period, and contain a mixture of garbled memories of Mycenaean times, contemporary features and pure invention which it is hard to disentangle with any confidence.

Other poets of the seventh and sixth centuries, such as Hesiod, Alkman and Sappho, wrote of the world they saw around them. This was one dominated by wealthy aristocratic families conspicuously displaying their wealth in their luxurious clothes, perfumes and jewellery.

Female dress

In the Archaic period the universal female garment seems to have been the *peplos*. This is also called the *heanos* by Homer but this may be a purely poetic term. The *peplos* was made from a rectangular piece of woollen cloth that was slightly taller than the wearer and more than twice the width of her body. To put it on (colour plate 2) the top was folded down, creating an overfold (*apoptygma*) which reached to about the waist. The *peplos* (figures 16 and 17) was then folded around the body and a piece of material (the *epomis*) was pulled forward over each shoulder and fastened to the front above the breasts with long pins or brooches. The double thickness of material created by the overfold may have helped to prevent the material ripping where it had been pinned. At the open side of the *peplos* one edge of the material was probably wrapped over the other and then fastened tightly in place with a girdle. This girdle, which would have helped to take some of the weight of the garment off the pins at the shoulders, was always worn. Alternatively the side may sometimes have been sewn shut and the *peplos* stepped into or drawn on over the head. The side may also have been closed with small brooches but this seems rather unlikely – on vases such brooches are never shown even where the pins at the shoulders are clearly visible.

The *peplos* is often shown as very richly decorated and is commonly described as *poikilos*, 'worked in many colours'. Floral, geometric and figured designs all appear (figures 17 and 18) and are similar to those on contemporary pottery. These designs probably derived originally from Phoenician and other eastern sources. Presumably, however, such elaborately decorated clothing was worn only by wealthy women. The poorer classes and slaves should be imagined dressed in garments of plain colours or of undyed wool.

16   Woman wearing a *peplos* fastened at the shoulders by long pins

17   Woman in a richly decorated *peplos*

Over the *peplos* a linen cloak or shawl was worn. Modern scholars usually call this a *himation* but it seems that this was probably a rather later generic term for 'cloak'. Homer and the other poets of the period refer to this garment as a *kredemnon, kalyptre* or *kalymma*. It varied in size and could be worn in a variety of ways. It was frequently draped over the shoulders like a shawl, with the ends falling over the arms and the front of the body left uncovered (figure 18). It might be drawn up over the head (figure 19) and could also be held over the face as a veil. In several cases two or more women are shown sharing a cloak. Sometimes it was worn wrapped around the body but this style was more favoured by men (see below and figure 22).

An alternative to the *kredemnon* was the *pharos*. From the poetic descriptions it seems that this was also made of linen and was a particularly large and luxurious garment worn only by the rich. It seems to have been worn in the same way as the *kredemnon*. Some sources, however, suggest that the *pharos* may also have been worn as a dress in the same way as the woollen *peplos*.

18　Woman wearing a cloak over her *peplos*

19　Woman wearing her cloak as a veil

18

19

Male dress

On vases of the period most men are shown wearing a tunic known as the *chiton*. Unlike the female *peplos* it seems that this was sewn rather than pinned. Certainly Homer talks of the *chiton* being 'drawn on' and does not describe it as being pinned, nor do pins or brooches ever appear in representations of it. It was probably woven as a long rectangular or slightly cruciform piece of cloth with a gap left in the centre for the head. It would then be folded in half and sewn up the sides either with holes left for the arms or with the cross piece forming short sleeves.

Older men and the better off wore an ankle-length *chiton* (figures 20 and 23), usually without a girdle. The poet Hesiod recommended a long *chiton* for winter wear. Younger men, and those engaged in more active pursuits, wore a thigh-length version (figure 21) which was usually held in place by a belt. The length of the *chiton* could be adjusted by pulling material up through the belt so that it hung over it in a small fold (figure 21). The *chiton* was frequently made of linen but it seems probable that wool which was both cheaper and warmer was used as well.

Men also commonly wore a wrap or cloak over the *chiton*. Sometimes indeed no *chiton* was worn and the wrap was the only garment (figure 22). The male cloak was generally described by contemporary writers as a *chlaina* although again the word *himation* is commonly used today. The *chlaina* was a warm, woollen garment worn by rich and poor alike and accordingly made in varying weights and textures.

20

20   Old man in a long *chiton* and *chlaina*

21   Young man in a short *chiton*

22   Man wrapped in a large *chlaina*

21

Two versions of the *chlaina* are mentioned, the *chlaina haploïs* ('single *chlaina*') and the *chlaina diple* ('double *chlaina*'). The single *chlaina* was sometimes worn wrapped around the body (figure 22). One end was hung forward from the left shoulder. The bulk of the garment was then drawn around the back and under the right arm. Alternatively it could be brought over the right shoulder, wrapping the right arm within it. The material was then taken across the chest and either thrown back over the left shoulder or draped over the left forearm. More commonly, however, the single *chlaina* was worn over the shoulders as a shawl in the same manner as the female *kredemnon* (figures 20 and 23).

The double *chlaina* (also known as a *diplax*) poses a problem. Homer describes it as being closed by a brooch but no brooch is apparent on any of the surviving representations. It seems most likely that it was a single *chlaina* folded in half and worn as a shawl in the way just described. The brooch could then have fastened it on the wearer's chest.

Men also wore the linen *pharos* which has already been described above. It was draped in the same way as the single *chlaina*.

23   Old man wearing a long *chiton* and *chlaina*

Another male garment was variously called the *zoma, diazoma* or *perizoma*. *Zoma* appears to have had several meanings depending on the exact context but Homer uses it of a kind of loin-cloth or kilt (figure 24) tied or wrapped around the waist. In poetry it is worn by athletes and by warriors below their armour and on vases versions of it are worn by athletes, craftsmen and labourers. It went out of use among athletes during the fifth century.

There is also some evidence that clothing made out of skins was worn. In the *Odyssey* there is a reference to a hairless deer skin being used as a poor man's cloak. Hesiod recommends the use of a cape made of kid skins as protection against the winter rains. However, the only skins shown on vases are those worn by gods, heroes and other mythological figures. These are usually fastened around the neck by knotting the paws together. It is unlikely that skins were actually worn in this way in real life.

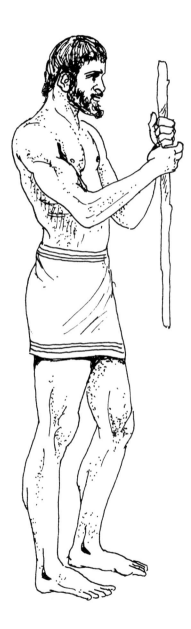
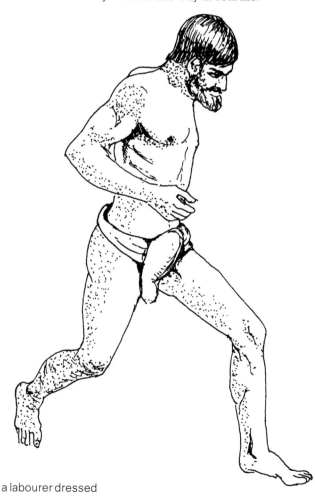

24   A runner and a labourer dressed in *zomata*

4 Female dress in the Classical Period:

The sixth and fifth centuries

By the end of the sixth century there was a clear reaction against the luxurious style of dress described in the previous chapter. The historian Thucydides attributed this to the influence of conservative Sparta and to a desire to render the gulf between rich and poor less blatant. This reaction against ostentatious living gained extra impetus after the Persian invasions of Greece in 490 and 480. Later in the fifth century we find the victorious Greeks drawing pointed contrasts between Persian softness and Greek austerity.

It should, however, be noted that the changes described here may have only affected limited areas. Our best information comes from Athens and it is clear that in other areas of the Greek world older styles continued for sometimes considerable periods after fashions had changed there.

Tunics

From c 540 Athenian women began to change from the *peplos* described in the previous chapter to the Ionic *chiton*. This was a much lighter linen garment adopted from the Greeks of Ionia (whence the name Ionic) although Herodotos maintains that the Ionians originally borrowed it from the Carians of Asia Minor.

The basic Ionic *chiton* (figure 25) was made from a rectangular piece of cloth. This was about as wide as the wearer when she stood with arms outstretched and slightly taller than her. It was folded into a cylinder which was sewn up at the side. The upper edge was then closed along the shoulders and upper arms by a series of small brooches or buttons (colour plate 4). Alternatively it might sometimes be stitched. Finally a girdle was tied around the waist, which pulled in the material and created long, baggy sleeves. The excess length was pulled up through the girdle to hang down in a kind of pouch (the *kolpos*) of varying size. Occasionally crossed cords were worn on the torso to hold the *chiton* in place (colour plate 4).

Although the *peplos* and the Ionic *chiton* co-existed for a time and were even worn together (see figure 29), with the *chiton* under the *peplos*, the *chiton* soon became the most popular garment among Athenian women and spread to other areas of mainland Greece. Herodotos tells a spurious but fascinating story of an Athenian expedition against the island of Aigina

25 Woman tying a girdle around an Ionic *chiton*

at some time in the early to middle sixth century. The expedition was wiped out but for one man. When the survivor reached home and broke the news the enraged women pulled the long pins from their *peploi* and stabbed him to death. The horrified Athenians supposedly punished their women by making them adopt the Ionic *chiton* which was not closed with long dress pins.

Early in the fifth century the *peplos* came back into fashion. It was a wider, fuller garment than before, made of lighter wool, simpler in style and frequently plain or with only coloured borders. The Dorian Greeks of the Peloponnese had continued to wear it during its time out of favour in Athens and it had become particularly associated with them. For this reason it was frequently called the Doric *chiton* rather than the *peplos*, although Herodotos always refers to it as an *esthes*.

It was put on and pinned at the shoulder (figure 26) as described in the previous chapter and was usually girdled at the waist. The overfold (*apoptygma*) tended to be longer than before, frequently long enough to hide the girdle, although its size did vary. One variety (figure 27), with a very long overfold and the girdle worn on top of the overfold, is known as the '*peplos* of Athena'. It is called this because it was the style used by the sculptor Pheidias on his famous statue of Athena Parthenos.

26 Woman wearing a Doric *chiton*

27 Woman wearing the '*peplos* of Athena'

26

27

The Doric *chiton* like the Ionic was usually sewn up at the side, occasionally with a decorated seam, but it might be worn open (*schistos*; figure 28). This was the way Spartan women wore it and the Athenians of the fifth century were scandalized because the Spartans also wore it without a girdle.

The two types of *chiton* were sometimes worn together again (figure 29) and soon began to influence each other. A number of varied styles are shown in surviving representations. Frequently the dress worn is so hybrid that it is difficult to tell whether it should be classed as Doric or Ionic. Some (figure 30) combine the pinning of the Ionic *chiton* with the Doric overfold. The Doric *chiton* might have some material pulled up through the girdle, creating an Ionic style *kolpos*. An incipient version of this can be seen on figure 27. Other varieties of tunic include an Ionic *chiton* with two girdles and two *kolpoi* (figure 31) and a Doric *chiton* (figure 29) showing two overfolds, one to the waist and the other to the breasts. One of these overfolds must have been sewn on to the *chiton* as a separate piece of material. Sometimes the Doric overfold at the back is pulled up over the head, like a veil.

Another type of tunic is occasionally seen worn over the *chiton* (figure 32). It was probably made from a long rectangular piece of material woven with a slit for the head in the centre. This was then folded in half and sewn up the sides, leaving holes for the arms.

The long-sleeved tunic (*chiton cheiridotos*) was considered rather un-Greek but examples do occur (colour plate 3). It was worn alone or with a *chiton* and was more commonly worn by women than by men. This too was made from one piece of material, this time woven in a cruciform shape. A slit for the head was again left in the centre. The material was folded in half and sewn at the sides and along the undersides of the sleeves.

We encounter the terms *chiton, chitonion, chitoniskos* and *chitonarion* in literary texts and inscriptions, but we do not know what distinguished one from another. It has been suggested that they might refer to variations in the fineness of the material or to the size of the dress but we do not know if these suggestions are correct. Similarly, we hear of women (and effeminate men) wearing a *krokotos* or *krokoton*, which was clearly a luxurious, saffron coloured garment of some sort, but we are not sure what it looked like.

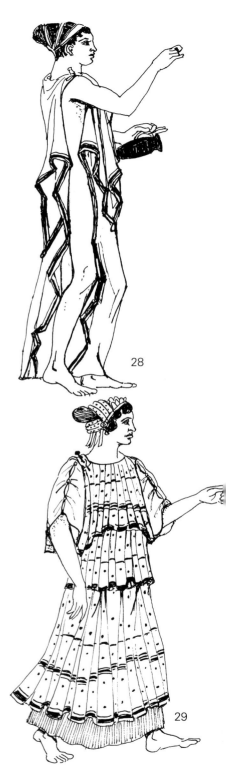

28   Woman in an ungirdled Doric *chiton* which is open at the side

29   Woman wearing a Doric *chiton* with an extra overfold over an Ionic *chiton*

30   Woman in an Ionic *chiton* with Doric style overfold

31   Woman in an Ionic *chiton* with two girdles

32   Woman wearing a sleeveless tunic over a *chiton*

33   Woman in a transverse *himation* over an Ionic *chiton*

Wraps

When outside of the house a Greek woman invariably wore a cloak or wrap over her tunic. This was always a simple rectangle of wool or linen of varying size and was worn in a variety of ways. Modern scholars tend to lump all such garments together under the term *himation*, which was probably a generic term for them. As we shall see later we know the names of a variety of wraps but we cannot identify specific ones in the surviving illustrations.

As described in the previous chapter the *himation* might simply be worn over the shoulders like a shawl. This is known as the 'symmetrical *himation*' (figure 18 and colour plate 4). In this case the *himation* was sometimes pulled up over the head.

More complex was the 'transverse *himation*' which was chiefly worn over the Ionic *chiton* (figure 33). Here the centre of the *himation* was placed over one hip. One end was brought across the chest, the other around the back and they were then pinned together along the shoulder (and sometimes the upper arm). Frequently the upper edge was rolled or folded down.

30

32

31

33

A large *himation* might be worn wrapped around the body (figure 34). One end would be hung forward from the left shoulder. The rest would then be brought across the back and either under the right arm or over the right shoulder and covering the right arm. It was then passed across the chest and either flung back over the left shoulder or draped over the left arm. To stop it slipping off the arm a fold of the *himation* was sometimes tucked into the girdle. In some instances the edge of the *himation* was folded down before putting it on. This created an overfold along the edge.

As already mentioned, we know the names of several kinds of wrap. The *chlanis* was made of particularly fine wool, that from Miletos being especially famous. The *xystis* was another fine wrap used on special occasions while the *ephestris* was similar to it but made of thicker wool. Others mentioned include the *ledos, ledarion, ampechonon* and *lope*.

Underclothes
We have almost no evidence about underclothes beyond some references to a soft band sometimes tied around the breasts. This was known (among other names) as a *strophion*. Representations of it are rare but on one vase a figure of Atalanta (figure 35), a mythological heroine, wears something not dissimilar to a modern brassiere. This is presumably an example of a *strophion*. She also wears a form of loin-cloth (*zoma*).

Entertainers and *Hetairai*
A number of representations of male drinking parties show female entertainers and *hetairai*, high class courtesans. Musicians and dancers may wear 'exotic' costumes (colour plate 3) or skimpy and revealing versions of the *chiton*. The *hetairai* are usually more modestly dressed but reveal their status by their presence at the parties where no respectable woman would have been found.

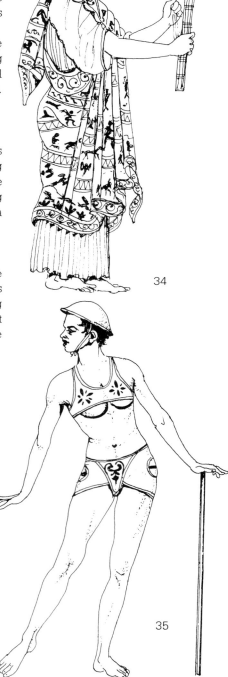

34

34 Woman wearing a *himation* draped over an Ionic *chiton*

35 Atalanta in *strophion* and *zoma*

35

5 Male dress in the Classical Period:

The sixth and fifth centuries

In the classical period Greek men wore clothes that were very similar to those of their womenfolk. Their dress was distinguished more by colour, material and size than by differences in the cut of the garments. Male fashions of this period followed the same trend as female, with simpler clothes replacing the richer garments worn earlier.

Tunics
All the varieties of tunics described in the preceding chapter were worn by men, although in slightly different forms. The Ionic *chiton* was worn in both long (ankle-length; figure 36) and short (to the thigh or knee; colour plate 5) versions. The long Ionic *chiton* tended to be worn by older men and also by others on religious or ceremonial occasions. It also became the standard garb for professional musicians (figure 37). This long version was known as the *chiton orthostadios* or *syrma*.

36   Man in a long Ionic *chiton* and *himation*

37   Musician dressed in a long Ionic *chiton*, playing a *kithara*

36

37

The male version of the Doric *chiton* (figure 38) appears only as a short garment reaching to the thigh or knee. It was worn without an overfold but was pinned at the shoulders in the same way as the female. A variant of it was the *exomis* (figure 39). This was pinned at the left shoulder only, leaving the right shoulder and breast bare. For this reason it was known as a 'one-armpit *chiton*' (*chiton heteromaschalos*) in contrast to the usual form which was classed as a 'two-armpit *chiton*' (*chiton amphimaschalos*). The *exomis* was the regular dress for slaves, craftsmen and labourers. The city of Megara was particularly famous as a centre for the manufacture of the *exomis*.

As well as tunics that were fastened with pins or brooches men also wore sewn tunics (figure 40). These were generally either sleeveless or had very short sleeves. Much more rarely they might have long sleeves. These tunics were woven in one piece and sewn up like their female counterparts described in the previous chapter.

Wraps

Men also wore a variety of rectangular linen or woollen wraps or cloaks when out of doors. Although the generic term *himation* is used today to describe most of them the Greeks themselves distinguished a variety of garments whose names we know but which we are unable to identify in the surviving representations. In the previous chapter we mentioned the *chlanis, xystis, ephestris* and others as being worn by Greek women. All of these were worn by men as well. In addition men also wore the *chlaina*, a thick woollen winter cloak, and the *ephaptis*, a more costly version of the *chlaina*.

The *himation* generally took the form of a large piece of cloth wrapped around the body (figure 41). One end was hung forward from the left shoulder. The remainder was brought around the back, under the right arm and across the chest. The other end would then be draped over the left arm or flung back over the left shoulder. An alternative arrangement was to bring the *himation* over the right shoulder rather than under the right arm. In this case the right arm would be enclosed in the *himation*. The *himation* could be worn over a tunic (figure 36) but was frequently the only article of clothing (figure 41).

There were definite points of etiquette and fashion involved in the correct draping of the *himation*. To let the hem trail on the floor was considered foppish and effeminate while to wear it with the left shoulder rather than the right shoulder uncovered was positively barbaric.

The 'symmetrical' and 'transverse' forms of the *himation* described in the previous chapter were not commonly worn by men.

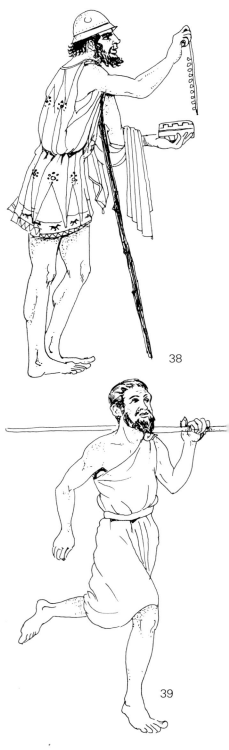

38 Man wearing a Doric *chiton* and felt hat (*pilidion*)

39 Man wearing an *exomis*

Another garment worn alone and wrapped around the body was the *tribon*. This was made of coarse dark-coloured wool and was the national dress of Spartan men. At Athens it was adopted by those with conservative, pro-Spartan leanings and later by philosophers. It remained the appropriate dress for the latter for centuries.

The *chlamys* was a slightly smaller cloak (figure 42). It seems to have originated in either Macedonia or Thessaly (where it was known as an *allex* or *allix*). It was usually worn over the left shoulder and fastened at the right shoulder by a pin or brooch part way along its upper edge. This left the right side of the body and much of the front uncovered. Alternatively it could be pinned at the throat (colour plate 5) so that it covered both shoulders.

The *chlamys* was the cloak typically worn by hunters and young aristocratic horsemen. Hunters are frequently depicted on Athenian vases (figure 42) and can be recognized by their *chlamys*, two javelins and felt hat (*petasos*). During the Hellenistic period the *chlamys* came to be worn by soldiers in particular.

40   Man in a sleeveless tunic

41   Man wrapped in a *himation*

42   Huntsman dressed in a *chlamys, chiton* and *petasos* (felt hat)

40

42

41

Another cloak favoured by horsemen was the Thracian *zeira* (figure 43; see chapter 9). This was a long, gaily patterned woollen cloak. It was often worn with Thracian style boots.

Each of the cloaks and wraps discussed so far was considered by the Greeks as a 'single cloak' (*haplegis*) as opposed to a 'double cloak' (*diplegis* or *diploïs*). 'Double cloaks' seem simply to have been folded in half to form a double thickness of material before they were put on. Where they can be recognized they appear (figure 44) to have been worn in the same manner as the *chlamys*.

43 Horseman wearing a *zeira*, *chiton* and *petasos*

44 Man in a 'double cloak'

PLATE 1 *Minoans and Mycenaeans*

PLATE 2 Woman, putting on peplos, and two men, c 600 BC

PLATE 3 *Entertainers and revellers enjoying a drinking party, c 500* BC

PLATE 4 *Family group of the early fifth century* BC

PLATE 5 *Fifth century* BC *street scene*

PLATE 6 Costume of the fourth century BC

PLATE 7 Group of soldiers of c 400 BC

PLATE 8 Performance of a phlyax *play, fourth century* BC

Other clothes

A number of representations show craftsmen, labourers and, presumably, slaves wearing the *zoma* (figure 45; colour plate 5). As described in chapter 3 this was a piece of cloth either tied around the loins or wrapped around the waist as a kind of kilt.

In the countryside it seems that the peasantry quite often wore clothes made of animal hides and skins, especially in the more backward areas of Greece. Pausanias, writing in the second century AD, mentions tunics of pig-skin being worn in Euboia and Phokis and we also hear of caps being made of dog-skin.

Among the garments named are the *dipthera*, a leather or goat-skin jerkin; the *sisyra* or *baite*, a goat-skin or sheep-skin cloak which was dressed with the hair still on; the *sisyrna*, which seems to have been the same as the *sisyra* but with the hair removed; and the *spolas*, a leather jerkin.

Unfortunately representations of skin clothing in art are largely confined to animal pelts tied around the shoulders of mythological figures. However, some representations do show men using skins as primitive shields (figure 66) and others show skin hats and cloaks (figure 46).

Finally we should mention a short-lived fashion for wearing headdresses and soft leather boots (*kothornoi*) which was introduced to Athens towards the end of the sixth century by the poet Anakreon of Teos (colour plate 3). This fashion originated among the Lydians of Asia Minor and first gained currency in Anakreon's native Ionia before he brought it to Athens. Because headdresses and *kothornoi* were normally worn only by women this fashion seemed positively effeminate to most Athenians.

45   Slave wearing a *zoma*

46   Shepherd dressed in a *chiton*, skin cloak (*sisyra* ?) and skin hat (*kyne*)

46

33

6 Post-Classical dress:

The fourth century and later

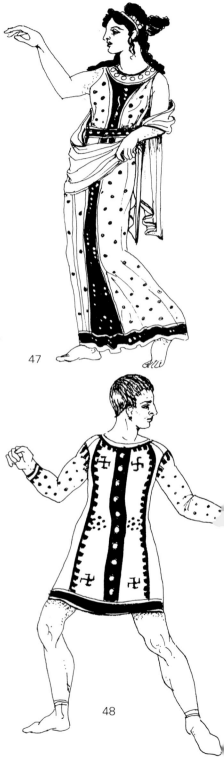

The period covered by this chapter falls naturally into two unequal parts. The first lasts for the first two-thirds of the fourth century, before the career of Alexander the Great. The second covers the Hellenistic period, the three centuries between 330 and 30, when Greek culture was spread around the entire east Mediterranean basin.

The fourth century

In this period both male and female costume seems to have remained basically similar to that worn in the fifth century. The various types of tunic continued in use, together with cloaks or wraps worn in an assortment of ways. However, the Doric *chiton* appears to have become less popular with men who tended rather to wear the sewn tunic (figure 48). The sewn tunic was also worn more commonly by women (figure 49), with the neckline often forming a shallow U or V. There was also a tendency for the girdle on the female tunic to be placed higher. Eventually it was normally tied below the breasts. This was especially true of the Doric *chiton* with a long overfold (the '*peplos* of Athena'; figure 50).

Vase paintings show female clothing becoming more highly decorated in this period (figure 47). They also suggest that the garments were made of thinner material and designed to cling to the contours of the body. However, it is likely that this reflects the painters' interest in the body and the flow of draperies across it rather than real life.

An inscription dating to the middle of the fourth century, found on the site of the Temple of Artemis at Brauron in Attica, records the garments stored in the temple treasury. It lists a series of tunics (*chitones*) which are differentiated by material, colour, decoration and presumably style.

Materials specified include hemp (*styppinos*), fine quality linen (*amorgis*) and carded wool (*kteniotos*). Colours include white, purple,

47

48

47   Woman dressed in a *chiton* and small *himation*

48   Young man in a richly decorated long-sleeved tunic

saffron-yellow, yellow, 'sea-green' (a blue-green) and 'frog-green' (a pale green). Garments could be striped (*pyrgotos*) or spotted (*katastikton*) while others are specifically described as 'decorated' or 'highly decorated', implying more complex designs. In some cases the tunics are said to have broad or narrow borders, sometimes of purple.

The epithets used to describe the style of the tunics are sometimes harder to interpret. A sleeved *chiton* (*chiton cheiridotos*) presents no problems but others are described as 'single' (*haploun*) or 'double' (*diploun*), which possibly refers to the absence or presence of an overfold. Other *chitones* are specifically defined as 'man's' or 'boy's'.

On vase paintings artisans and labourers continue to be shown wearing the *zoma* (figure 51), either as a loin cloth or as a wrap-around kilt.

49   Woman wearing a Doric *chiton* over a short-sleeved tunic and a veil

50   Woman wearing a Doric *chiton* with a long overfold

51   Workman dressed in a *zoma* and *pilidion*

49

50

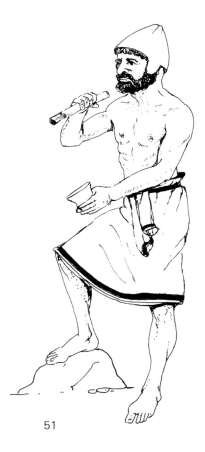

51

The Hellenistic Period

The tradition of pottery painted with figured scenes comes to an almost complete stop at the end of the fourth century. We are therefore forced to fall back on other much less satisfactory sources of information for the next three centuries.

The evidence from literature is scanty, consisting mainly of passing references, and is often difficult to interpret. Turning to the visual arts, there are few wall paintings or mosaics earlier than the first century. Much of the sculpture of the period consists of nudes or of figures dressed in a very stereotyped way. In addition sculptors often looked back to the works of earlier centuries and imitated or adapted them. In the second and first centuries this trend became even stronger thanks to the growing power and wealth of the Romans and their demand for copies of Greek works of art. This leaves as our richest source of information the thousands of terracotta figurines produced in this period. Even with these it is often hard to pick out details of the clothing worn and the female figures frequently wear a standardized combination of *chiton* and draped *himation*.

Bearing these limitations in mind it would seem that by and large the older forms of clothing survived, although they must have developed in ways that we cannot now closely follow. Both the Doric (figure 52) and the Ionic *chiton* appear on female statues. Although it is always possible that this reflects the copying of fifth century originals we must presume that it also mirrors contemporary styles. Certainly a lady called Praxinoa (who appears in a third century poem by Theokritos) wears one *chiton* at home and prepares to go out by putting on a second *chiton*, which is fastened at the shoulder by pins or brooches. Over these she puts on a wrap, specified in the poem as an *ampechonon*. Nevertheless, it is clear that the sewn tunic continued to grow in popularity with women (figure 53).

The terracotta figurines show women wearing the *himation* in a number of ways. By far the most common style (figure 53) is that where one end of the *himation* is hung forward over the left shoulder while the rest is brought around the back, around the right side, across the chest and then either thrown back over the left shoulder or draped over the left arm. Often (figure 54) the body is completely swathed in the *himation*, with both arms enclosed, the head covered and even the face veiled. Alternatively the *himation* may simply be tied around the hips (figure 52) leaving the arms free. More rarely the *himation* might be draped over the shoulders like a shawl (figure 55).

Men's tunics were now generally sewn rather than pinned (figure 56). Short or long sleeves became much more common in this period. Over this tunic they might wear a *himation*, wrapped around the body in the way just described, or a *chlamys*, pinned at the right shoulder (figure 56). The draped *himation* also commonly appears as the only garment worn (figure 56).

52 Woman in a Doric *chiton* with her *himation* tied around her waist

53 Woman wearing a short-sleeved tunic and *himation*

54

In the Hellenistic period there were Greeks living throughout an area that stretched from Sicily to India and from the Crimea to Egypt. They settled in particularly large numbers in the countries bordering the eastern Mediterranean. One result of this expansion was the creation of an increasingly standardized and cosmopolitan culture throughout the area as Greeks from different regions of Greece were mixed together and also found themselves living among a variety of foreign peoples. This was reflected in the clothing of the period. Many foreign garments were adopted, such as the *mandya*, a form of cloak or wrap; the *kapyris*, a sleeved robe; and the *sarapis*, a Persian robe. Unfortunately we do not know precisely what these garments looked like.

Late in the second century and in the first century the growing dominance of the Roman Republic over the Greek states saw an increase in the appearance of Roman fashions in the Greek world. Roman dress is covered in a companion volume of this series.*

Costume of Ancient Rome, D J Symons, Batsford 1987

54   Woman swathed in a large *himation* and wearing a *tholia* on her head

55   Woman in a *chiton* with her *himation* around her shoulders

56   Man dressed in a short-sleeved tunic and *chlamys* (left) and another in a *himation* (right)

55

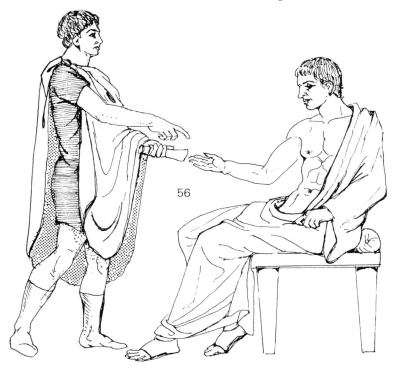

56

7 Military costume

After the collapse of the Mycenaean civilization we have very little evidence for military dress until the eighth and seventh centuries. At that time we can start to piece together information from a number of sources to build up a coherent picture.

The Archaic Period

Archaeological finds, especially from graves, provide us with painted vases and terracotta and bronze figurines that represent warriors as well as with sporadic examples of armour and weapons. At first the figures on vases are highly stylized (figure 57) but they become more realistic in the seventh century. Literary sources, especially Homer's *Iliad* (probably composed in the later eighth century), contain much information on warfare but are difficult to interpret (see chapter 3). Using these sources we can reconstruct the appearance of a soldier of the wealthy classes (figure 58).

Body armour consisted of the 'bell' cuirass, so called today from its shape. This was made of bronze breast and back plates (*gyales*) and came down to the waist. From some representations it is clear that it could be highly decorated. An eighth century specimen found in a grave at Argos had the plates hinged together at one side and buckled at the other. Sometimes a semi-circular bronze plate was hung from a belt below the cuirass to protect the abdomen (figure 58).

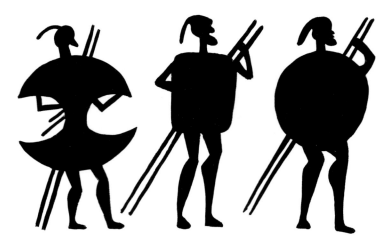

57 Stylized figures of eighth century warriors with assorted types of shields

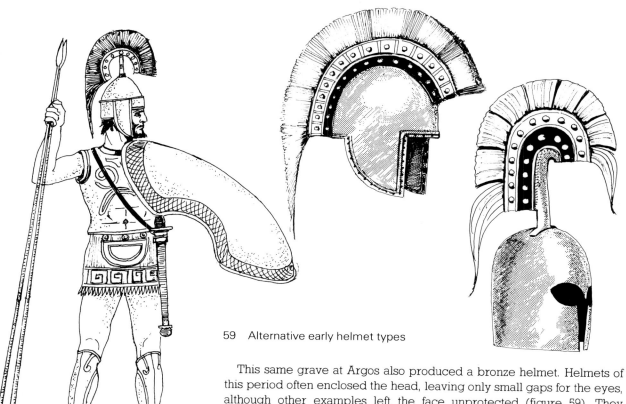

59   Alternative early helmet types

58   Aristocratic warrior of the eighth century wearing a bell cuirass.

This same grave at Argos also produced a bronze helmet. Helmets of this period often enclosed the head, leaving only small gaps for the eyes, although other examples left the face unprotected (figure 59). They frequently had a horsehair crest, sometimes raised on a tall crest-holder, to increase the wearer's height and make him look more terrifying. Stitched or glued inside the helmet was a lining made of leather, linen, felt or a kind of sponge called *achilleios*. This was designed to make the helmet more comfortable and to give greater protection against blows. Sometimes a skull-cap of similar material was worn under the helmet (colour plate 7).

Further protection was given by greaves and a shield. The greaves were made of bronze (figure 58) and usually had a lining similar to that of the helmet. A roll of this lining was often placed at the base of the greave to stop it chafing the ankle. Early greaves were highly decorated and covered only the lower leg. They were held in place by straps or by their own elasticity.

Representations on eighth century vases show three types of shield – round, rectangular or 'hour-glass' (figure 57). Of these the hour-glass or Dipylon type (figure 58) is by far the most commonly illustrated although the indentations in the sides are clearly exaggerated by the painters. Homer describes these shields as made of a wooden or wickerwork frame covered with layers of leather, sometimes with an outer facing of bronze. They were light enough to be hung from the shoulder by a strap, leaving both hands free. They could also be held by a hand-grip in the centre of the shield.

A warrior's weapons consisted of two throwing spears, a sword (*xiphos*) and a dagger (*encheiridion*). The sword was a two-edged cut and thrust type and was suspended at the left hip by a leather baldric.

In the Homeric poems battles were primarily clashes between aristocratic warriors armed in this way. Backing them up were lower class fighters armed with bows, javelins or slings. Painted vases and Homer's descriptions suggest that chariots were used in the fighting but it is virtually certain that this is not so. They probably represent a 'heroic' element based on faint memories of Mycenaean war chariots. Instead it seems that the aristocrats used horses as transport and occasionally as cavalry mounts (figure 60), although they probably usually fought on foot.

The Hoplite

By the early seventh century a new type of shield had been introduced. This was the *hoplon* (figure 61), a large, heavy, round shield that covered its holder from the neck to the thigh. It was made of a wooden core with a bronze facing and a leather lining. The arm was thrust through a central armband (*porpax*) and the hand grasped a hand-grip (*antilabe*) near the edge of the shield. A cord running around the interior may have allowed the shield to be carried on the back rather like a knapsack. The interior was sometimes strengthened with a metal reinforcing plate to give the arm added protection. A thick leather or cloth flap (figure 63) might be suspended from the *hoplon* to protect the legs. The outer face of the *hoplon* was painted with a design intended to intimidate the enemy and identify the bearer (colour plate 7).

60 Light cavalryman of the seventh century

61 Hoplite wearing linen body armour

62 Hoplite wearing a bronze muscle cuirass

63 Hoplite with scale-covered linen armour and a flap attached to his shield

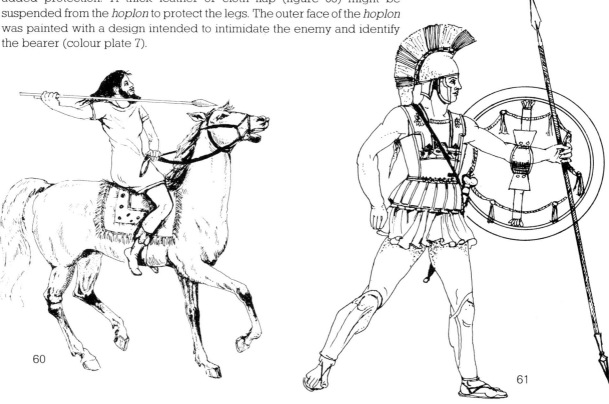

60

61

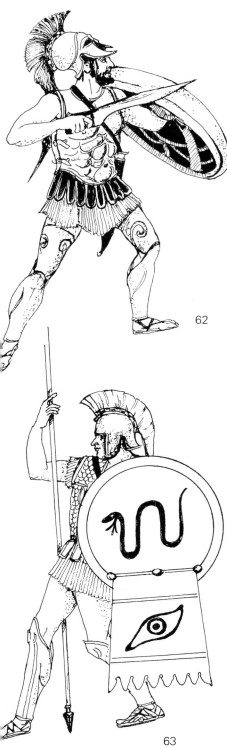

62

63

During the seventh century the use of the *hoplon* and the adoption of a long spear that was used for thrusting rather than throwing led to a change in the nature of warfare. Instead of duels between aristocratic champions, battles were fought by opposing armies each ranged in a phalanx, a formation eight rows deep and as long as numbers allowed. Great discipline was required to keep tightly to the formation as each man's right side was partly protected by his right-hand neighbour's shield. In battle two opposing phalanxes charged at each other and a pushing and stabbing match ensued until one side or the other broke and ran.

This new type of infantryman was known as the hoplite (*hoplites*), from the *hoplon* which he carried, and he dominated Greek warfare from the late seventh to the fourth century (figures 61, 62 and 63). As well as the *hoplon* his defences commonly consisted of a helmet, cuirass and greaves.

During this period greaves were less highly decorated and came to be modelled on the muscles of the leg. They were also made longer so that they covered the knee. Helmets similar to those worn earlier continued in use but more open types also came into fashion during the fifth century (colour plate 7).

The bell cuirass continued to be worn into the later sixth century but it was eventually replaced by the lighter and more flexible linen cuirass (figure 61). This was made up of a large number of layers of linen glued together until the required thickness was reached. The lower part was split into two layers of flaps (*pteryges*) arranged so that the upper layer covered the gaps in the lower. This arrangement allowed the wearer greater freedom of movement. The linen cuirass was put on by wrapping it around the body and tying it at the left side (colour plate 7). A U-shaped piece was fixed to the back and the uprights were pulled down over the shoulders and fastened on the chest. In some cases (figure 63) the linen cuirass was strengthened by the addition of scales or plates, probably of metal.

During the fifth century another type of bronze body armour appeared. This is known as the 'muscle' cuirass from the way it reproduces the musculature of the naked male torso (figure 62). It was an expensive item and came to be favoured by officers. It either ended at the waist or was prolonged to protect the abdomen. Generally *pteryges* were attached to its lower edge.

Other pieces of armour are known from scenes on vases or from actual finds. They include bronze protectors for the upper arms and forearms, heels and ankles and the feet. The thighs were sometimes protected by bronze or leather pieces called *parameridia* (figure 62). All of these items were unusual and they seem to have gone out of use among hoplites by the fifth century at the latest.

The hoplite carried a thrusting spear (*dory, enchos*). This was two to three metres in length. It had a spiked butt which could be stuck in the ground but which also doubled as a weapon if the spear shaft broke. In addition he carried a sword, still worn at the left hip. This was initially the straight two-edged *xiphos* (figure 61), about 60 cm long. In the late fifth and fourth centuries it was made shorter. At the same time a different form of sword also became popular. This was a curved single-edged slashing sword (figure 62) called the *kopis* or *machaira*.

Cavalry and other infantry

As well as hoplites a Greek army of the late seventh to fourth centuries included cavalry (figure 64) and more lightly equipped infantry. Cavalry were mainly used as scouts and guards and as skirmishers to harass the enemy and pursue them if they were beaten. The only part of mainland Greece really suitable for cavalry was Thessaly. Other states, however, also maintained small cavalry forces and there is evidence that these were being increased from the middle of the fifth century onwards. Cavalry of this period seem to have been equipped in a variety of ways. Some wore helmets of various kinds and body armour (figure 64) while others wore no armour at all. Shields seem to have rarely been carried. Cavalry weapons included the bow, javelins and a long spear (the *xyston*), as well as a sword. Xenophon, writing in *c* 360, recommended that cavalrymen should have (figure 64) armour for the left arm and the thighs and a helmet allowing all-round vision and should carry javelins and the *kopis* slashing sword.

64   Cavalryman wearing bronze body armour, a helmet and limb protectors

65   Cretan archer

65

64

66 Stone thrower

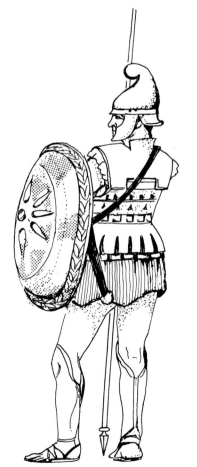

Light infantry consisted of men armed with bows, javelins or leather slings which fired stones or almond-shaped lead shots. The poorest even appear to have fought armed only with stones or cudgels. Archers and slingers were found in all armies but the inhabitants of certain areas were particularly proficient and were frequently in demand as mercenaries. For example, Crete was famous for its archers (figure 65) while backward areas like Akarnania and Achaia used the sling (colour plate 7). Such troops seem generally not to have worn armour and to have worn leather or felt hats rather than helmets. Cretan archers seem to have been unusual in that there is some evidence that they used small bronze shields. Stone throwers (figure 66) are often shown using an animal hide as a rudimentary shield.

Light javelin men (colour plate 7) were known as peltasts from their shield, the *pelte*. This consisted of a wooden or wickerwork frame covered by leather or skins. Its shape is uncertain. Most representations show it as an oval with a semi-circular 'bite' from one side but other evidence suggests it was round or rectangular. It was much smaller and lighter than the *hoplon*. Peltasts also carried a sword. They became more important in warfare in the fourth century after the Athenian general Iphikrates and a force of peltasts wiped out a unit of Spartan hoplites at Lechaion in 390.

The Hellenistic Period

The army developed by Philip II and Alexander the Great of Macedon established a new pattern which lasted throughout the Hellenistic period. In place of the hoplite phalanx there was a new phalanx 16 ranks deep consisting of men called phalangites (figure 67) armed with the *sarissa*, a pike 5.5 to 6.5 m long. The men in the front ranks wore fairly heavy armour, probably muscle cuirasses or linen strengthened with metal plates. The others wore either linen cuirasses or possibly no body armour at all. Because both hands were needed to grasp the *sarissa* the shield was made with a much shallower curvature than the hoplite shield so that the *sarissa* and the shield-grip could both be held in the left hand. The phalangites also wore greaves and helmets which seem to have sometimes been painted for unit identification. Several helmet types were in vogue including one with a high peak. In addition to the *sarissa* a sword was carried, the curved *kopis* being more popular than the straight *xiphos* at this period.

The phalanx was supported by various light infantry of the kind already described and by a range of armoured and unarmoured cavalry armed with the *xyston*, javelins or bows.

67 Macedonian phalangite of the late fourth or third century

8   The Theatre

Theatrical performances were very popular among the Greeks from the fifth century onwards. They were held in open-air theatres, usually built into a hill-side. The spectators sat in tiered rows of seats facing a circular dancing-floor (*orchestra*) and a small stage (*skene*). Plays were performed only at certain times of the year, during religious festivals sacred to the god Dionysos. They developed in Athens in the sixth century from earlier choral performances in Dionysos' honour. To a modern eye the strangest features of an ancient Greek theatrical performance would have been the masks worn by the actors and the presence of a chorus who sang and danced as an integral part of the play. Furthermore all parts were played by men.

There were several kinds of drama, each with its own appropriate costumes which will be discussed below.

68   Tragic actor playing a female role

Tragedy

According to later tradition tragedy was invented by an Athenian called Thespis in the years after 550. Tragic plays were performed by two or three actors and a chorus of 12 to 15 men. The plays usually drew on mythology for their themes which were always serious in nature. In Athens in the fifth century tragedies were performed in a theatrical competition as part of the festival of Dionysos. Three playwrights competed each year. Each one had to produce three tragedies and a satyr play (see below) which were staged one after another on the same day. The greatest tragic playwrights were Aeschylus (*c* 525-456), Sophocles (*c* 496-406) and Euripides (*c* 485-406). Although tragedies were still written in the fourth century the Greeks of that day themselves thought the works inferior and frequently revived the works of these earlier masters.

A tragic play might include as many as ten characters. Each actor might therefore have to play several parts. The different characters were indicated by different masks but the actor wore the same costume throughout the play. Both male (figure 70) and female (figure 68) characters wore a *chiton* with long sleeves. Generally this was floor-length but for certain characters (such as soldiers) it reached to about the knee (figure 69). In the fifth and fourth centuries the *chiton* was girdled around the waist but in Hellenistic times the belt was placed higher, just below the breast. One form of *chiton* worn by female characters was the *syrma* which had a train attached. Over the *chiton* the actor wore either a *himation* (figure 68)

69   Tragic actor playing a soldier

70 Tragic actor holding his mask

or a *chlamys* (figure 69) or some other form of cloak. All of these clothes were richly decorated in what was essentially a survival of the luxurious styles normal in the sixth century.

To increase his height the actor wore *embates* or soft boots with thick wooden soles (figure 69). The *embates* were made so that they fitted either foot. With time the wooden soles grew much thicker and it required great skill to learn to walk on them. To further exaggerate the proportions of the body padding was worn below the *chiton*.

Later tradition maintained that Thespis was the inventor of the theatrical mask. He is said to have first used white lead on the face, then to have used cinnabar or wine lees, and finally to have used a linen mask. Aeschylus is said to have brought the mask to its final form. The mask was made to cover the whole head (figures 70 and 71a) and not just the face. It was tied below the chin with bands. Rising above the face was a tall frame (the *onkos*; figure 71d) which was covered by the mask's hair and further raised the actor's height.

Our evidence for fifth century masks suggests that they were quite simple (figure 71b). Later they became much more elaborate with the features distorted and the mouth gaping wide (figures 71c,d). Pollux, a writer of the second century AD, gives us a list of mask types which he probably took from a Hellenistic source. This list describes 28 varieties of tragic mask, distinguished by the colour and style of the hair, the colour of the face and by details of the facial features. Each had a special name and was appropriate for a particular kind of character. For example, the *anasimos* ('snub-nose') had a high forehead, fair hair, red face and no beard. It was one of the masks used to represent a slave. It is, however, doubtful if masks were quite so systematized in the fifth century.

The members of the tragic chorus also wore masks like those of the actors. Because they needed to dance they usually wore a shorter version of the *chiton* (figure 69) with a *himation* as well as shoes called *krepides* rather than the actors' *embates*. If the play required it they might also wear special dress. For example, we know that when Aeschylus' *Eumenides* (*The Kindly Ones*) was first put on the chorus of avenging spirits was dressed in black, with horrific masks.

Where the plot or the character required, both actors and chorus might carry props. For example, a king might hold a sceptre or Herakles his club.

(a)

71 (a) Tragic actor with mask of a hero, (b) young woman's mask, (c) old woman's mask, (d) old man's mask

(b)

(c)

(d)

Satyr plays

The satyr play was something of a light relief after the three tragedies that preceded it. Although not strictly a comedy, the satyr play certainly had a farcical side. It was usually based on a mythological theme which it freely parodied. It takes its name from its chorus. This was made up of satyrs – wild and mischievous half-human beings with snub-noses, pointed ears and tails who provided the rowdy element in the plot.

The actors' dress was like that already described for tragedies. The twelve members of the satyr chorus, however, (figure 72) wore *somatia*, a tight flesh-coloured ensemble that covered the arms, legs and torso and simulated the naked body. Around the groin they wore a kilt or apron (*perizoma*) made of goat-skin with a horse's tail and a leather phallus attached. Their masks were designed to reproduce the snub-nose and pointed ears of the satyr.

At some time late in the fifth century or early in the fourth the chorus leader came to represent Pappasilenos (figure 73), the father of the satyrs, a drunken but clever old fellow. His costume usually consisted of *somatia* decorated with tufts of goat's hair or made completely of goat-skin.

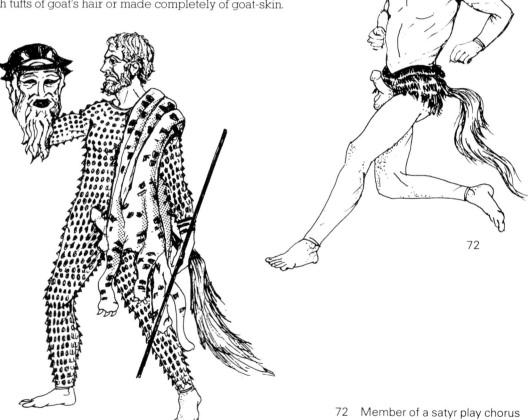

72

73

72   Member of a satyr play chorus

73   Actor playing Pappasilenos, with his mask removed

Comedy

Comedy developed later than tragedy and was first performed in Athens at the festival of Dionysos in 486. Each year at the festival five comedies, each by a different author, were performed in the course of a single day. (During the Peloponnesian War the number was temporarily reduced to three.) Later Greeks divided comedy into Old, Middle and New Comedy.

Old Comedy (fifth century)

In Old Comedy, political, social and literary themes were used as a vehicle to lampoon well-known Athenians in an incredibly scurrilous fashion. The plays, which would seem extremely crude and vulgar to a modern audience, concentrated on the creation of fantastic and ludicrous situations. The greatest writer of Old Comedy was Aristophanes (*c* 445-385).

The actors (probably three but possibly as many as five in developed Old Comedy) were given a deliberately grotesque appearance. They wore (figure 74) flesh-coloured *somatia* heavily padded at the stomach and buttocks. Over these came a *chiton* or *exomis* cut very short to show a large leather phallus with a red tip which was attached to the *somatia*. In addition to or instead of the *chiton* a *himation* might be worn (see figure 77). Female characters generally wore a long *chiton* but some might appear 'nude' or 'semi-nude' in which case the *somatia* were appropriately padded and details were painted on to them. Because comedies tended to be more energetic affairs than tragedies comic actors wore a variety of everyday shoes and boots rather than the tragic actors' *embates*. Comic actors' masks (figure 74) either represented stock types such as 'a slave' or 'a farmer' or they were wicked caricatures of real people.

The chorus of 24 was also masked. They were often dressed like the actors in *somatia, chiton* and *himation*. However, as in tragedy, where the play demanded it they could be given special masks and costumes (figure 75), as in Aristophanes' *The Birds*.

74 Old Comedy male character

75 Chorus members playing cavalrymen in an Old Comedy play

Middle Comedy (c 400-330)

Our knowledge of Middle Comedy is rather poor but it seems to have been characterized by a reduction in the role of the chorus and a greater use of stock characters. Subjects tended to be drawn from mythology and the tragic plays rather than from real life. Our evidence for Middle Comedy costume comes mainly from the terracotta statuettes of comic actors that became common at this period. These suggest that the costume just described for Old Comedy continued in use but with its grotesque elements more exaggerated (figures 76 and 77).

New Comedy (c 330-250)

New Comedy was moralistic rather than satiric. The old vulgarity disappeared, together with the fantastic situations. Its place was taken by a comedy of manners, drawn from contemporary life and with the emphasis on an elaborately involved plot. By this time the chorus was used only to link the scenes played by the actors. The finest exponent of New Comedy was the Athenian Menander (c 343-291).

The costume of the New Comedy actor (figure 78) was closer to that of real life. The leather phallus disappeared and, although the actor still wore *somatia*, so did the grotesque padding except for slave characters. For male parts the actor now wore either a long or a thigh-length *chiton*, sometimes with a *himation* or *chlamys*, and for female ones a long *chiton* with a *himation*. Garments of particular colours were appropriate for certain types of character – for example, young men wore red and young women white. There was also an appropriate mask for each stock character (figure 79). Pollux lists 44 different types. Most were ridiculous, with widely gaping mouths, and those for slaves were particularly grotesque.

Phlyax plays

Phlyax plays evolved in the Greek cities of southern Italy and Sicily. They were produced (colour plate 8) without a chorus, using only actors. From the start they were parodies of myths, daily life and (later) tragic plays. *Phlyax* (the name means 'babbler') scenes were very popular subjects on local vases from the end of the fifth century to the end of the fourth.

The *phlyax* actor's costume was similar to that of Athenian Old Comedy with padded *somatia* plus phallus, *chiton* or *exomis* and *himation* being worn.

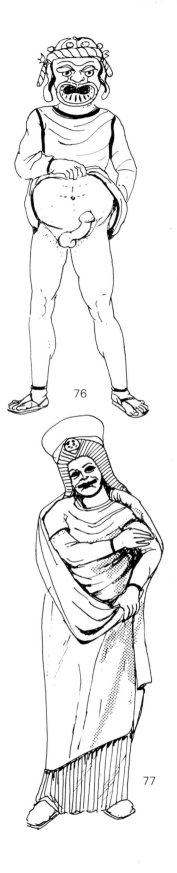

76 Middle Comedy actor playing a male part

77 Middle Comedy actor playing a female part

78   New Comedy actors playing (a)
a father, (b) a soldier and (c) a slave

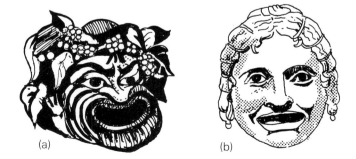

79   New Comedy masks of (a) a
slave and (b) a young woman

9   Foreigners

Both in their homeland and as a result of their expansion around the shores of the Mediterranean the Greeks came into contact with many peoples of very different cultural backgrounds. In many cities of Greece itself we have evidence for communities of metics (*metoikoi*), resident aliens who were generally involved in trade and industry. It has been estimated that there may have been as many as 25,000 metics in Athens in the late fifth century. Most of these were citizens of other Greek states but others were certainly 'barbarians' (ie non-Greek). It is likely that long residence in Greece led many metics to adopt Greek dress. The man shown in figure 80, with his decidedly un-Greek features, is probably a Syrian or Phoenician resident in Athens in the closing years of the sixth century. He is wearing a *himation*. In their homelands these foreign peoples wore their native dress which was very different to that of the Greeks. In the remainder of this chapter we will look briefly at some selected examples of the classical Greeks' contemporaries.

Thracians

The Thracians were a warlike people who lived in the area covered by the modern Bulgaria, European Turkey and north-eastern Greece. They were divided into a number of tribes each ruled over by a king and aristocracy. According to the historian Herodotos the warrior class despised agricultural labour and considered the only respectable sources of wealth to be war and plunder. He also says that tattooing was a mark of high rank and this is seen on Thracian women in Greek depictions of them.

The Greeks became familiar with the Thracians with the establishment of Greek colonies along the north Aegean coast from the seventh century onwards. From the start there were periodic hostilities and Greek appreciation of Thracian fighting qualities led to their frequent employment as mercenaries. The most famous example of this is an incident recorded by the historian Thucydides. In 413, during the Peloponnesian War, the Athenians hired 1300 Thracians who gained great notoriety for their particularly brutal sacking of the small Boiotian town of Mykalessos.

Other Thracians came to Greece as slaves. On Greek vases Thracian women are generally shown as nursemaids and are recognisable by their tattoos. Other, mythological scenes show them murdering Orpheus, a legendary poet and singer. In each case they are shown in Greek dress,

80   Phoenician or Syrian resident in Athens

probably reflecting the vase painters' familiarity with them as slaves in the city (figure 81).

Thracian men, naturally enough, are shown as warriors. Typically (figures 82 and 83) they wear a long boldly patterned woollen cloak (*zeira*) over a short tunic, although the soldier and historian Xenophon describes the tunic worn in winter as long enough to cover the thighs. On their feet are high leather boots, laced up the front and with tongues of a fur or felt lining folded down over the top of the boots. Thracians were particularly known for their fox-skin headdress, the *alopekis*. This had long ear-flaps and a neck cover which was sometimes made of cloth. The ear-flaps might be tied up above the head (figure 82). In some instances the *alopekis* was made from the skin of the fox's head. The eye-slits and ears are clearly visible in figure 82. Other examples are made from plain fur (figure 83) or, to judge from the patterning on them, from some other kind of hide or fur (figure 84).

As warriors, Thracians usually carry a pair of javelins and a *pelte*, a light oval shield with a circular 'bite' out of one side (figure 83).

81   Tattooed Thracian woman

82   Thracian warrior wearing a *zeira* and *alopekis*

83   Thracian warrior showing his tunic and shield

82

83

Scythians

The Scythians were a nomadic people who lived to the north of the Thracians. Their main centre was in southern Russia but they extended as far west as Hungary and similar peoples inhabited the steppes as far east as Siberia. The Greeks encountered them when the citizens of Miletos founded colonies on the northern shores of the Black Sea towards the end

84   Thracian wearing a hide headdress

85   Scythian archer

86   Scythian stringing his bow

of the seventh century. Relations were generally friendly and a flourishing trade soon grew up. In addition, Scythian slaves became known in Greece itself. The Athenians, after 480, maintained a force of public slaves known as the 'Archers' or 'Scythians'. This was initially 300 strong (later increased to 1200) and its members acted as a kind of police force, maintaining public order and attending on government officers.

Herodotos describes the closely related Sakai, who were subjects of the Persian Empire and served in the Persian army, as wearing trousers and tall pointed hats and carrying a bow, dagger and axe (*sagaris*). This is basically the costume which we find Scythians wearing in Greek depictions of them (figures 85 and 86). In addition to tight trousers, often tucked into leather boots, they wear a long-sleeved, tightly fitting jacket girdled at the waist. This jacket is usually shown wrapped across the chest and ending at the hips. On their heads are tall felt caps normally with long ear-flaps. Herodotos, in his description of Scythian customs, also tells us that they scalped their defeated enemies and, if they accumulated sufficient scalps, would sew them together to make a cloak.

From Greek sources, and from some remarkable discoveries made in contemporary Siberian tombs, we know that Scythian clothing was richly decorated. It was brightly coloured in strong reds, blues, greens and yellows and, in addition, small metal plaques in the shape of stylized animals might be sewn on to it. Scythian clothing was produced from leather, felt, wool and hemp.

The Scythians were expert archers, usually using the bow from horseback. They are normally shown with a bow and a combined bow-case and quiver known as a *gorytos* (figure 85). In time Greek artists came to depict archers, Amazons and orientals in Scythian dress.

Lydians

In Asia Minor the Greeks had long been in contact with a number of peoples of whom the Lydians may stand as representatives. Early in the seventh century the Lydians created a kingdom, based on their capital at Sardis, which came to dominate western Asia Minor. By the sixth century they had brought many of the Greek cities of the coast under their control. Fifth century Greek writers maintained that it was the Lydians who introduced 'luxury' to the Greeks via Ionia. Certainly Lydian styles had an impact on Athens in the late sixth century (see chapter 5; colour plate 3). In 546 Croesus, the last king of Lydia, was defeated by Cyrus of Persia and Lydia was incorporated into the Persian Empire.

Figure 87 shows an offering-bearer from the Persian royal palace of Persepolis. Although not all the figures in these sculptures are securely identified it is very probable that this is a Lydian. Herodotos tells us that Lydian troops in Xerxes' army were dressed and equipped like Greeks and this is reflected here. The figure wears a long tunic and cloak wrapped

87   Lydian offering-bearer from Persepolis

around the body in the style of a Greek *himation*, very like the costume worn by the man in figure 36. On his feet are boots typical of Asia Minor and on his head a banded conical hat. One peculiarity to be noted is the long lock of hair falling behind the ear.

Phoenicians

The Phoenicians (and their Canaanite forebears) inhabited the coast of modern Syria and Lebanon. They were a cosmopolitan people, well-known to Homer and later Greeks as skilled craftsmen and great traders. Their trading and colonising took them the length of the Mediterranean. Cyprus and Sicily were occupied by both Greeks and Phoenicians and the Phoenicians also settled at Carthage in Tunisia and in Sardinia, Corsica and the Balearics.

In the sixth century Phoenicia was absorbed into the Persian Empire and Phoenician ships served in the Persian navy against the Greeks. The Carthaginians also fought a series of wars in their own right against the Greeks of Sicily. However, both Phoenicians and Carthaginians were very open to progressively stronger Greek influence.

Native Phoenician dress seems to have consisted of a long, close-fitting tunic with short sleeves. A shorter tunic sometimes seen may be a separate garment or the long version girded up for easier movement. The clothes were made of wool or linen and were brightly coloured and richly decorated. Figure 88 is taken from the stele of Baalyaton, a priest of Tyre, and dates to the third century. His long tunic is fairly loose, reflecting Greek influence, and is probably of linen. Over this he wears what seems to be a cloak fastened at the chest and girdled at the waist to form large baggy pseudo-sleeves. The low round cap appears to have been a priestly accessory.

Persians

The people probably most commonly associated with the Greeks are the Persians. From their original home in southern Iran the Persians, under their kings Cyrus (559-29), Cambyses (529-22) and Darius (522-486) conquered an empire that stretched from the Aegean to India. In 490 and 480 they launched invasions of Greece. They were defeated on both occasions but they retained control of Asia Minor and remained a potential menace until their empire was taken over by Alexander the Great (336-23).

The conquest of western Asia Minor and Cyprus brought Greeks under Persian rule. This, and the two invasions of Greece, meant that Greeks knew of the Persians primarily as soldiers and rulers. To reflect this two figures of Persian soldiers drawn from the palace at Persepolis are illustrated here. Figure 89 shows a soldier dressed in the so-called 'robe of honour', a loose flowing garment. On his head is the Persian fluted felt hat.

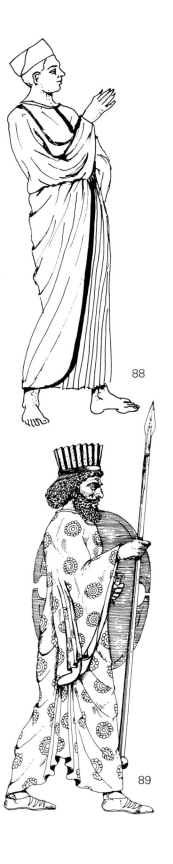

88

89

88   Phoenician priest

89   Soldier from Persepolis in Persian costume

Figure 90 is dressed in the costume of the Medes, a closely related people who lived in northern Iran. This consisted of tight-fitting trousers and a long-sleeved, thigh-length tunic and is topped off by a felt cap. Median costume was clearly more practical for warriors and Herodotos states that Persian soldiers in fact wore tunic and trousers on active service. They were armed with a light wickerwork shield (figure 89), bow, spear, and short sword (*akinakes*).

It is interesting to compare the Persian representations with the way Athenian vase painters depicted Persians in the years after 480 (figure 91). They showed the rich decoration on the clothes, on which Herodotos comments, but tended to make the clothes looser and more flaring. They usually represented the tunic in such a way that it looks as if it is sleeveless and worn over a body-stocking. The headgear also looks more Scythian than Persian.

Neither illustration shows armour being worn. However, Herodotos specifically mentions that the Persians wore scale body armour. In addition, a conical bronze helmet, dedicated by the Athenians at the Temple of Zeus at Olympia, is inscribed as being part of the spoil won from the Persians.

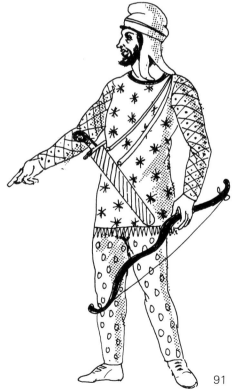

90   Soldier from Persepolis in Median costume

91   Greek depiction of a Persian soldier

10 Accessories

(a)

In this final chapter we will look at certain aspect of dress which, while not all strictly articles of clothing, do allow us to form a more detailed picture of the appearance of the Greeks.

Female hairstyles

Most women wore their hair long. Only slaves or women in mourning had it cut short. In the seventh and sixth centuries it was commonly worn falling over the shoulders and down the back (figure 92a) and was usually fastened by a headband (*mitra, tainia, anadesme*). This was frequently accompanied by a *stephane* or *ampyx*, a crescent-shaped metal diadem worn over the forehead (see figure 92f). Towards 500 the hair began to be restrained, with the ends either gathered into a small bag (figure 92b) or tucked up under the headband (figure 92c).

(b)

In the fifth and earlier fourth centuries it was more common for the hair to be worn up. The vases and sculptures show us an enormous variety of styles. In many cases the hair was tied or pinned into a bun. This was usually coupled with a simple headband (figure 92d), a more complex arrangement of bands (figure 92e) or a *stephane* (figure 92f).

Alternatively the hair might be wrapped in a *sakkos*, a length of material wound around the head and then secured. This frequently completely covered the hair except for the fringe (figure 92g), a few curls by the ears (figure 92h) or a tail end of hair hanging behind (figure 92i). The *stephane* was also worn with the *sakkos*. A simpler smaller version of the *sakkos* was the *sphendone*. This was also wound around the head but covered less of the hair (figure 92j).

(d)

(e)

(f)

(c)

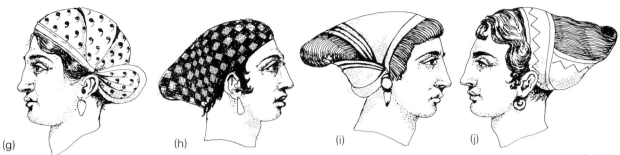

(g)   (h)   (i)   (j)

92   Female hairstyles

(a)

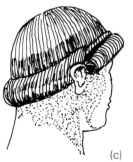

(b)

In the Hellenistic period the *sakkos* and the *sphendone* seem to have been abandoned. Instead the hair was artificially waved and curled into a variety of styles. It was, however, still normal for the hair to be worn up.

In addition to the hairdressing aids already mentioned the Greeks also used hair nets made by a warp-plaiting technique known as sprang. Wigs and hairpieces, known variously as *fenakai, entricha, penikai* or *prokomia*, were worn by men and women alike. Dye was also used either to darken grey hairs or to achieve a fashionable blonde.

Male hairstyles

In the Homeric poems and the art of the seventh and sixth centuries free men (but not slaves) wore their hair long, usually with a headband (*mitra*) to hold it in place (figure 93a). The *mitra* might also be used to hold the hair up as in figure 92c. Alternatively, in the early fifth century, the hair might be rolled up and tucked tightly over the headband (figure 93b) or be twisted into two plaits which were wound around the head and fastened together over or under the fringe (figure 93c).

From the late sixth century short hair (figures 93d and e) became more and more common, especially among younger men, although older men continued to wear their hair long well into the fifth century. Long hair remained common for boys even later than that. Among the idiosyncratic Spartans this was reversed – there boys wore their hair short and adults let theirs grow.

(d)

(e)

93   Male hairstyles   (c)

Short hair remained the norm until the late fourth century when Alexander the Great (figure 93f) set a fashion by wearing his hair a little longer, so that it was compared to a lion's mane. From the third century hair was once again worn shorter.

Alexander also introduced one specific form of headband. This was the *diadema* (figure 93g), a white band worn with the ends hanging loose behind the head. This had been one of the royal attributes of the Persian kings. After conquering Persia Alexander adopted the *diadema*, which became the normal symbol of royalty in the Hellenistic period.

Until the fifth century it was normal for men to wear a beard (*pogon, geneion, hypene*), usually but not always with a moustache (*mystax*) (figure 93a). A moustache was never worn alone. Youths and young men, however, are often shown as beardless (figures 93b and c).

During the later fifth century and for most of the fourth the wearing of a beard was a matter of personal taste (figures 93d and e). Alexander the Great was clean-shaven (figure 93f) and this became the norm in the Hellenistic period. Although certain individuals (figure 93g) cultivated beards it was never very common to do so.

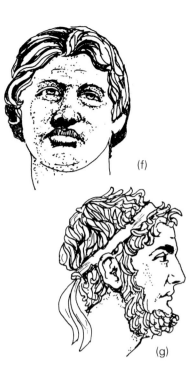
(f)

(g)

93   Male hairstyles

Cosmetics

A variety of cosmetics and perfumes were frequently used by women and sometimes by men as well. The complexion was whitened to a fashionable pallor with white lead (*psimythion*). This was prepared by leaving lead to corrode in vinegar, scraping off the corrosion product and powdering and heating it.

The cheeks were reddened with rouge (*phykos*) which was produced from a number of sources. These included seaweed, *anchousa* made from the root of the ox-tongue or bugloss, *paideros* made from an unidentified flower and *sykaminon* made from crushed mulberries.

Finally the eyebrows and eyelids could be blackened with sulphuret of antimony (*stimmis*) or *asbolos*, a preparation made from soot.

Perfumes were used on both the skin and hair. They were generally oil-based and scented with flowers or blossoms such as roses.

Jewellery

Greek jewellery was made in a variety of materials. Gold, silver and bronze were commonly used but lead, iron, bone, ivory and glass are also known. It was decorated by techniques including cutting, chasing, inlaying, filigree and granulation.

Jewellery was largely a female preserve except for finger rings (*daktylioi*) which men also wore both for use (as seals) and for ornament. Rings might be made entirely of metal or might have paste or a stone set into them. The Spartans, with their reputation for austerity, were said to wear iron rings.

Earrings (*enotia, ellobia, hermata*) were very commonly worn by women. They generally took the shape of discs, rings or hooks with pendants. Necklaces (*hormoi*) consisted of beads in a variety of materials

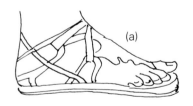
(a)

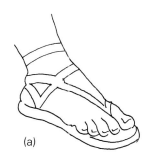

(a)

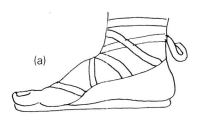

(a)

(b)

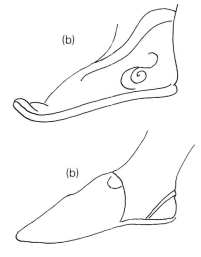

(b)

(b)

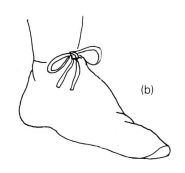

(b)

either strung together or hanging as pendants from a band around the neck.

Bracelets (*pselia*) were a favourite ornament and were worn on one or both arms, either at the wrist or on the upper arm or both. In addition, an anklet (*periskelis*) might be worn.

Finally, the pins (*belonai*) and brooches (*peronai*) used to fasten clothing were often ornaments as well as serving a practical function.

Footwear

At home, and often outside, Greeks of all classes went barefoot much of the time. However, a variety of footwear was also worn. This was usually made of leather from the hides of cattle. Alternatively softer, finer shoes and boots were produced from the skins of calves, sheep and goats by a process known as tawing, where alum rather than tannic acid was used in the curing process. This resulted in a naturally white leather. Other colours such as red and yellow were produced by dyeing but the leather was often left its natural colour or blackened.

In addition to leather felt was used to produce warm boots and we know of wooden shoes called *kroupezai*. Wood sometimes also replaced the layers of leather normally used to form the soles.

Footwear was roughly divided into sandals (*sandalia, pedila, hypodemata*), shoes (*hypodemata koila*) and boots. Although ancient authors tell us the names of many varieties of these it is virtually impossible to identify those named with those represented on sculptures and in vase paintings.

Sandals (figure 94a) consisted of soles strapped to the feet, the straps sometimes carrying on a little way up the leg. One type, known as 'dusty feet' (*konipodes*), were obviously of light construction. Probably similar were *blautai*. More luxurious were the white *phaikades*, the *peribarides* and the 'Etruscan sandals' (*sandalia Tyrrhenika*) which had rectangular wooden soles.

Shoes (figure 94b) were made in the same way as sandals but had all or part of the foot enclosed in leather uppers. Some had an upper formed of a number of segments held together by straps. Typical of these were *krepides* which came in a stout nail-studded version for soldiers and a lighter version for women. Other light shoes were named after their places of origin – *Lakonikai* from Lakonia, *Argeiai* from Argos and *Rhodiakai* from Rhodes. What distinguished one from another we do not know.

Other shoes were loose-fitting and more closely resembled our slippers. Examples included *diabathra*, the yellow kid-skin *eumarides* and the white *Persikai*.

94 Footwear

Horsemen and hunters often wore boots reaching up the calf. These are generically described as *embatai*. They might be lined with felt or fur for extra warmth or softness and, in many cases, tongues of this lining can be seen hanging down from the top of the boot (figure 94c). *Endromides* seem to have been boots that were laced up rather than pulled on.

Some boots were named after particular people, like the *Iphikratides* and the *Alkibiades* named after Athenian generals. *Kothornoi* formed part of the costume of tragic actors (see chapter 8) but were usually worn by women. They had rectangular soles and could fit either foot. Cheap hard-wearing working boots were known as *arbylai* or *pelopatides* ('mud-treaders').

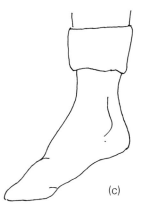

(c)

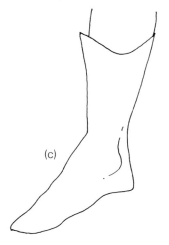

(c)

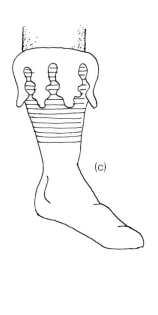

(c)

(c)

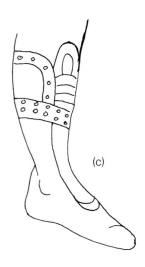

(c)

94   Footwear

(a)

(b)

95   Men wearing *pilidion* and *kyne*

Hats

When travelling, or in hot or wet weather, the Greeks often wore hats or pulled a fold of the *himation* over their heads (figures 19 and 54).

Hats were usually made of felt (*pilos*). *Pilos* is often used by modern scholars to describe a conical felt hat (figures 35, 38, 51 and 95a) but it seems that this should more correctly be called a *pilidion* and that *pilos* was used to cover all hats made of felt. We know of various types of *pilidia* named after their places of origin (for example, Arkadian, Lakonian and Macedonian) but we do not know their distinguishing features.

Another felt hat was the *petasos* (figures 42, 44 and 96), which supposedly derived from Thessaly. This had a more or less broad rim and a strap to hold it in place. This strap might be worn below the chin or around the nape of the neck (figure 43). The brim was often cut into a decorative shape and could be turned up or down. In its earliest form it is regularly turned up at the back (figure 96a).

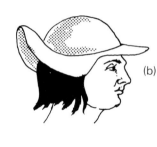

(b)

(c)

(a)

(d)

(e)

96   Men wearing *petasoi*

When goddesses are portrayed in art they are often shown wearing a hat known as a *polos* (figure 97a). This was cylindrical in shape and probably made of metal. However, it is very unlikely that it was ever an article of everyday dress.

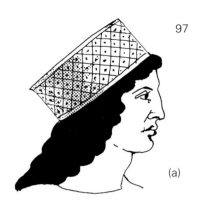

(a)

In addition to felt, hats of skin or leather (*kynai*) were also worn (figures 46 and 95b). These can only be recognized in surviving representations when their markings clearly show them to be made of skin. They are not often found but when they do occur they are usually similar in shape to the *pilidion*.

During the Hellenistic period two other types of hat came into vogue. The *tholia* was a flat broad-brimmed hat with a tall pointed crown (figures 54 and 97b). It was probably made of straw and was worn as a sun-hat, particularly by women. The *kausia* was of Macedonian origin and was made of felt (figure 97c). Macedonian and Hellenistic kings wore a purple *kausia* as a mark of royalty.

Miscellaneous accessories

Fashionable women, at least from the fifth century onwards, might carry a parasol (*skiadeion, skiadiske*) to protect them from the sun (figure 98). These were made of cloth stretched over a wooden frame. Another female accessory was the fan, made either from feathers fixed to a handle or from cloth over a frame. Fans varied in size from ones small enough to hold in the hand (*rhipidion*; figure 99) to the large variety (*rhipis*) which had to be operated by a slave (colour plate 3).

(b)

Men commonly carried a stick of some kind (*bakteria, rhabdos, skeptron*; figures 23, 38 and 41, colour plate 4). This might be plain and straight or have a curved head or it could be highly ornamented. Men also carried a purse (*marsippion*) since, among the upper classes at least, it was they who did the shopping while their wives stayed discreetly at home. The purse was a leather pouch with a drawstring around the mouth and was often attached to the belt. The *ballantion* was a larger satchel usually slung around the neck (figure 100).

97 Women wearing (a) a *polos* and (b) a *tholia* and a man (c) in a *kausia*

98 A parasol (*skiadeion*)

99 A fan (*rhipidion*)

100 A satchel (*ballantion*)

(c)

Further reading

98

99

100

ABRAHAMS, E B and Lady Evans, *Ancient Greek Dress*, London, 1964

BALDRY, H C, *The Greek Tragic Theatre*, London, 1974

BIEBER, M, *History of the Greek and Roman Theatre*, Yale, 1961

BOARDMAN, J, *Athenian Black Figure Vases*, London, 1974

BOARDMAN, J, *Athenian Red Figure Vases: The Archaic Period*, London, 1975
(Boardman's books are useful sources of illustrations).

BURN, A R, *The Pelican History of Greece*, Harmondsworth, 1974
(Good, one volume historical introduction to the period).

CONNOLLY, P, *The Greek Armies*, London, 1977

COOK, R M, *Greek Painted Pottery*, London, 1960

HAVELOCK, C M, *Hellenistic Art*, New York, no date (1960s?)

HIGGINS, R A, *Greek and Roman Jewellery*, London, 1961

HIGGINS, R A, *Greek Terracottas*, London, 1967

HOUSTON, M G, *Ancient Greek, Roman and Byzantine Costume*, London, 1947

LEVI, P, *Atlas of the Greek World*, Oxford, 1980
(Informative on most aspects of Greek life).

RICHTER, G M A, *A Handbook of Greek Art*, London, 1965
(Excellent general survey of the subject)

RICHTER, G M A, *The Sculpture and Sculptors of the Greeks*, Yale, 1970

WARREN, P M, *The Aegean Civilizations*, Oxford, 1975
(Useful guide to the Bronze Age in Greece)

Index